The Drucker Foundation Self-Assessment Tool

PARTICIPANT WORKBOOK

Revised Edition

Peter F. Drucker

Foreword by Frances Hesselbein

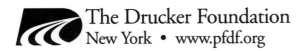

The Drucker Foundation
New York • www.pfdf.org

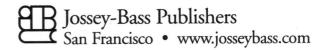

Jossey-Bass Publishers
San Francisco • www.josseybass.com

Jossey-Bass books and products are available through most bookstores. To contact Jossey-Bass directly, call (888) 378-2537, fax to (800) 605-2665, or visit our website at www.josseybass.com.

Substantial discounts on bulk quantities of Jossey-Bass books are available to corporations, professional associations, and other organizations. For details and discount information, contact the special sales department at Jossey-Bass.

ISBN: 0-7879-4437-8

This book is printed on paper containing a minimum of 10 percent postconsumer waste and manufactured in the United States of America.

Interior design by Gene Crofts

PB Printing   10 9 8 7 6 5 4 3 2   SECOND EDITION

Contents

Foreword   v
Frances Hesselbein

Acknowledgments   viii

About Peter F. Drucker   ix

PART ONE

Introduction to Self-Assessment

Self-Assessment: The First Action Requirement of Leadership   3

How to Use This Workbook   7

Definition of Terms   9

120653

PART TWO

The Five Questions

QUESTION 1   What Is Our Mission?   13

    WORKSHEET 1   What Is the Current Mission?   17

    WORKSHEET 2   What Are Our Challenges?   18

    WORKSHEET 3   What Are Our Opportunities?   19

    WORKSHEET 4   Does the Mission Need to Be Revisited?   20

QUESTION 2   Who Is Our Customer?   21

    WORKSHEET 5   Who Are Our Primary and Supporting Customers?   25

    WORKSHEET 6   How Will Our Customers Change?   26

QUESTION 3   What Does the Customer Value?   31

    WORKSHEET 7   What Do We Believe Our Primary
    and Supporting Customers Value?   35

    WORKSHEET 8   What Knowledge Do We Need to Gain from
    Our Customers?   36

    WORKSHEET 9   How Will I Participate in Gaining This Knowledge?   38

QUESTION 4   What Are Our Results?   39

    WORKSHEET 10   How Do We Define Results?   45

    WORKSHEET 11   Are We Successful?   46

    WORKSHEET 12   How Should We Define Results?   48

    WORKSHEET 13   What Must We Strengthen or Abandon?   49

QUESTION 5   What Is Our Plan?   51

    WORKSHEET 14   Should the Mission Be Changed?   57

    WORKSHEET 15   What Are Our Goals?   58

Afterword: Effective Implementation of the Plan   59

About the Drucker Foundation   62

Self-Assessment Tool Customer Feedback Form   64

Foreword

Remarkable opportunities exist for those who would lead their enterprises and this country into a new kind of community—a cohesive community of healthy children, strong families, good education, decent housing, and work that dignifies. In this period of unprecedented worldwide societal transformation, these leaders will dare to see life and community whole. They will strive to address the needs of the spirit, the mind, and the body. They will view their work as an amazing opportunity to express everything within that gives passion and light to living, and will have the courage to lead from the front on issues, principles, vision, and mission that become the star to steer by.

Self-assessment is a discussion about the future and how your organization will shape it. It is an intellectual and emotional adventure—for minds and hearts are involved. Rather than fret about a "shrinking piece of the old pie," nonprofit organizations with vision and new mind-sets will forge relationships crossing the private, public, and social sectors to build partnerships and community. They will welcome the challenge of accountability, define and achieve meaningful results, and articulate their accomplishments in a way that draws interest, energy, and support to their mission. They will *change lives*.

The demand that social sector organizations show results is not a passing trend. Nor should it be. The demand today and for the future is *performance*. The first requirement of volunteers, partners, and funders at all levels is to see that a difference is being made. They are asking, *How are you changing lives and communities for the better?* In this environment, self-assessment is vital.

If Peter Drucker were to sit down with your nonprofit organization, he would ask, *"What is our mission? Who is our customer? What does the customer value? What are our results?* and *What is our plan?"* He would ask these five questions because they go to the very heart of an organization, why it exists, and how it will make a difference. They are the five most important questions because they are the *essential* questions. One self-assessment participant called them "sharply pointed as a bayonet," and by asking them, you will focus on excellence in performance and what you must do to achieve it. The questions are not easy. We members of the Drucker Foundation board and staff ask them of ourselves periodically, and I know when *you* ask these questions, all who participate in seeking answers will have an exuberant and valuable discussion.

This must be a *three-way* conversation that includes the board, staff, and your customers. In the self-assessment process we ask that you go directly to those you serve, to your volunteers, your partners, and supporters, and let their insights influence your own. How you think about results and how you innovate and change will be immeasurably enriched. When board members, staff, and your customers together shape the mission and the goals, you create an organizational direction with passion and energy behind it that carries you even further than you can imagine.

To be able to say "We are successful, we are furthering the mission," a social sector organization must continually appraise its performance. This revised edition of the *Drucker Foundation Self-Assessment Tool for Nonprofit Organizations* is the result of such an appraisal. In the four years following its initial publication in 1993, more than ten thousand social sector organizations purchased the *Tool,* and many wrote or spoke with us about their experience with the self-assessment process. We heard the *Tool* was a success, that using it did indeed deepen an organization's sense of purpose and help to define its goals. And we heard invaluable suggestions for how the *Tool* could be improved. We wanted to understand what changes were needed, so we followed up with a nationwide survey, in-depth interviews, and focus groups, and we field-tested potential revisions.

Our customers told us they needed more guidance in adapting the *Tool* to their particular setting, to streamline the Participant Workbook, to underscore the importance of listening to *their* customers, to clarify and sharpen the planning process, and to provide additional insights from Peter Drucker on how to successfully implement a plan. We are deeply grateful for the response to our questions and the opportunity to use the ideas of those with firsthand knowledge of what is valued: our customers.

We also learned of the *Tool*'s great flexibility. It is used by organizations in all three sectors, serves as a university-level teaching tool, and is in the reference libraries of nonprofit executives and management support organizations. Portions of it are adapted and woven into a range of planning exercises. The *Tool* guides the work of leadership teams, the board chairman, and chief executive officer. It is used by individuals and by giant organizations, management teams, and small project teams, as well as by large partnership groups.

We welcome your use of the *Tool* however it best serves *you*. Please adapt the self-assessment process to the needs and culture of your organization. *Make it your own.*

The mission of the Drucker Foundation is *to lead social sector organizations toward excellence in performance.* We have no greater expression of this mission than the *Self-Assessment Tool.* The *Tool* is an adventure in organizational self-discovery, a means for assessing how to *be*—how to develop quality, character, mind-set, values, and courage. It begins with questions and ends with action. To quote a customer, "It has only one purpose: to put the organization on track. And it works." On behalf of the Drucker Foundation, I welcome and encourage you on this journey into the future.

August 1998

Frances Hesselbein
President and CEO
The Peter F. Drucker Foundation
for Nonprofit Management

Acknowledgments

We are deeply grateful, first and foremost, to the hundreds of nonprofit executives, facilitators, and other customers who shared their experience and comments on the first edition of the *Self-Assessment Tool* and thereby helped us to improve it. Our thanks again go to Constance Rossum for her original work on the self-assessment process and to the many individuals who contributed to the *Tool's* original development. Our appreciation also goes to Steven Gray for customer research, to Alan Shrader, our editorial partner at Jossey-Bass, to Rob Johnston, for his skillful guidance of this project, and to Gary J. Stern, who edited and field-tested this revised edition. Our final thanks go to the foundation's honorary chairman, Peter F. Drucker, for his decades of dedication to the effective organization, for his contributions to management literature, and for his support and contributions to the social sector.

Development of the revised *Drucker Foundation Self-Assessment Tool* was made possible in part by financial support from the GE Fund.

About Peter F. Drucker

Peter F. Drucker is a writer, teacher, and consultant specializing in strategy and policy for businesses and social sector organizations. He has consulted with many of the world's largest corporations as well as with nonprofit organizations, small and entrepreneurial companies, and with agencies of the U.S. government. He is the author of twenty-nine books, which have been translated into more than twenty languages, and has made several series of educational films based on his management books. He has been an editorial columnist for the *Wall Street Journal* and contributes frequently to the *Harvard Business Review* and other periodicals.

Drucker was born in 1909 in Vienna and was educated there and in England. He took his doctorate in public and international law while working as a newspaper reporter in Frankfurt, Germany. He then worked as an economist for an international bank in London. Drucker came to the United States in 1937. He began his teaching career as professor of politics and philosophy at Bennington College; for more than twenty years he was professor of management at the Graduate Business School of New York University. The recipient of many awards and honorary degrees, Peter Drucker has, since 1971, been Clarke Professor of Social Sciences at Claremont Graduate University.

Peter Drucker has been hailed in the United States and abroad as the seminal thinker, writer, and lecturer on the contemporary organization. In 1997, he was featured on the cover of *Forbes* magazine under the headline, "Still the Youngest Mind," and *BusinessWeek* has called him "the most enduring management thinker of our time."

PART ONE

Introduction to Self-Assessment

Self-Assessment: The First Action Requirement of Leadership

A Time to Shape the Future

Nonprofit institutions are central to the quality of life in America and central to citizenship; indeed, they carry the values of American society and the American tradition. The social sector organization has been America's resounding success in the last fifty years, whether we talk of institutions like the American Heart Association, which has taken leadership on major health issues, or of youth services such as the Girl Scouts of the U.S.A., or of the recovery techniques of Alcoholics Anonymous, or of the fast-growing synagogues, churches, and mosques, or of the community developers that have revitalized urban neighborhoods, or of outstanding museums and colleges, or of the many other nonprofit groups that have emerged as the center of effective social action in a rapidly changing and turbulent America.

We are living through a period of sharp transformation. People born fifty years from now will not be able to imagine the world into which their own grandparents were born. Society is rearranging itself—its worldview, its basic values, its social and political structure, its arts, its key institutions. Social sector organizations will be needed even more urgently in the next decades as needs grow in two areas. First they will grow in what has traditionally been considered *charity*—helping the poor, the disabled, those who suffer deprivation, the victims of violence or disaster. And they will grow, perhaps even faster, in services that aim to *change the community and to change people.*

What new questions will arise and where the big new issues will lie, we can, I believe, already discover with some degree of probability. In many areas we can also describe what will not work. But answers to most questions are still largely hidden in the womb of the future. What the future society will look like depends on leaders in all sectors and on each of us in our work and life. This is a time to *shape the future*—precisely because everything is in flux. This is a time for self-assessment, clear-minded decisions, and, above all, a time for action.

The Search for Community, Commitment, and Contribution

Every other American adult—90 million people all told—works at least three hours a week as "unpaid staff," that is, as a volunteer with a nonprofit organization. By the year 2010, the number of such unpaid staff people should have risen to 120 million, and their average hours of work to five per week. The main reason for this upsurge of volunteer participation in the United States is not the increase in need. The reason is the search for community, for commitment, and for contribution. Again and again when I talk to volunteers, I ask, "Why are you willing to give all this time when you are already working hard?" Again and again I get the same answer, "Because here I know what I am doing. Here I contribute. Here I am part of a community."

The nonprofit organization is a new center of meaningful citizenship, of active commitment. It offers the means to make a difference in one's community, one's society, one's own country, and beyond. Citizenship in and through the social sector is not a panacea for the world's ills, but it may be a prerequisite for tackling these ills. The organizations of the social sector have the critical leadership challenge to restore civic responsibility and the civic pride that is the mark of community.

Focus on Results

All social sector organizations share the common "bottom line" of *changed lives*. This is where *results* are—in the lives of people outside the organization—and achieving these bottom-line results is of absolute importance. Forty-five years ago, when I first began working with nonprofit organizations, many felt that good intentions were enough. "Business" subjects such as management, marketing, and return on investment were almost never discussed. Today, nonprofits have to think through very clearly what results are for their organization. They must demonstrate both commitment *and* competence in a highly demanding environment. People are no longer interested to know, "Is it a good cause?" Instead, they ask, "What is being achieved? Is this a responsible organization worthy of my investment? What difference is being made in society, in this community, in the life of individuals?" The successful nonprofit institution will hold itself accountable for performance inside the organization—for effective marketing, exemplary management of human and financial resources, for contribution in all areas—but always with the central focus on its one bottom line: changed lives.

The Five Most Important Questions

When we announced in 1990 that we were establishing the Peter F. Drucker Foundation for Nonprofit Management, many in the social sector approached me, along with Frances Hesselbein and members of our board, saying, "The most important management resource we need is a method to help us think through what we are doing, why we are doing it, and what we *must* do." And so we developed this *Self-Assessment Tool,* which presents the five most important questions for any nonprofit organization to ask: *What is our mission? Who is our customer? What does the customer value? What are our results? What is our plan?*

The questions are straightforward—and deceptively simple. Throughout the self-assessment process, you will examine the fundamental question of your mission: what the mission is and what it *should* be. You will determine your *primary customer:* the person whose life is changed through your work. You will determine your *supporting customers:* volunteers, partners, donors, and others you must satisfy. You will engage in research to learn directly from customers what they value, decide what your results should be, and develop a plan with long-range goals and measurable objectives.

Encourage Constructive Dissent

All the first-rate decision makers I've observed had a very simple rule: If you have quick consensus on an important matter, don't make the decision. Acclamation means nobody has done the homework. The organization's decisions are important and risky, and they *should* be controversial. There is a very old saying—it goes back all the way to Aristotle and later became an axiom of the early Christian Church: In essentials unity, in action freedom, and in all things trust. Trust requires that dissent come out in the open.

Nonprofit institutions need a healthy atmosphere for dissent if they wish to foster innovation and commitment. Nonprofits must encourage honest and constructive disagreement precisely because everybody is committed to a good cause: Your opinion versus mine can easily be taken as your good faith versus mine. Without proper encouragement, people have a tendency to avoid such difficult, but vital, discussions or turn them into underground feuds.

Another reason to encourage dissent is that any organization needs its nonconformist. This is not the kind of person who says, "There is a right way and a wrong way—and our way." Rather, he or she asks, "What is the right way *for the future?*" and is ready to change. Finally, open discussion uncovers what the objections are. With genuine participation, a decision doesn't need to be sold. Suggestions can be incorporated, objections addressed, and the decision itself becomes a commitment to action.

Creating Tomorrow's Society of Citizens

Your commitment to self-assessment is a commitment to developing yourself and your organization as a leader. You will expand your vision by listening to your customers, by encouraging constructive dissent, by looking at the sweeping transformation taking place in society. You have vital judgments ahead: whether to change the mission, whether to abandon programs that have outlived their usefulness and concentrate resources elsewhere, how to match opportunities with your competence and commitment, *how you will build community and change lives.* Self-assessment is the first action requirement of leadership: the constant resharpening, constant refocusing, never being really satisfied. And the time to do this is when you are successful. If you wait until things start to go down, then it's very difficult.

We are creating tomorrow's society of citizens through the social sector, through *your* nonprofit organization. And in that society, everybody is a leader, everybody is responsible, everybody acts. Therefore, mission and leadership are not just things to read about, to listen to; they are things to *do* something about. Self-assessment can and should convert good intentions and knowledge into effective action—not next year but tomorrow morning.

How to Use This Workbook

The *Self-Assessment Tool* was intentionally developed as a flexible resource. How you use this book will depend on your setting and the particular purpose for which self-assessment is being undertaken. The Workbook has not arrived on your doorstep on its own. It is in your hands because you have an interest in it or an Assessment Team, an instructor, a manager, or leader has thought through a self-assessment process design, identified a role for you, and asked you to participate. It is the responsibility of that team or individual to explain the purpose for self-assessment and to orient you to specific time and task expectations.

The self-assessment process calls for broad participation to ensure understanding, ownership, and readiness to act. Certain adaptations of the self-assessment process are discrete and may be completed within a matter of weeks. Comprehensive self-assessment for a nonprofit organization takes place in three phases over a number of months. A detailed Process Guide shows those leading self-assessment how to properly organize and direct it.

This Workbook has a twofold purpose: *(1) to guide your individual thinking and (2) to prepare you and others for productive discussion and decision making.* To make the most of what is offered here you will do three things.

1. Thoroughly review the information that is provided on your organization, its customers, trends in its operating environment, and other self-assessment materials or reports.
2. Sit down with this Workbook and, in one or more sessions, take the

necessary time to read it through and give a thoughtful response to the important questions it asks.

3. Actively participate in a retreat, group discussions, a one-to-one depth interview, or in other self-assessment meetings.

The Workbook contains introductory passages on the five questions, which are followed by sets of worksheets. The passages are intended to help your exploration by providing theory, insight, and pertinent examples. These examinations build on one another to create a whole. You may wish to read the entire Workbook before you answer any questions, or you may enjoy discovering each challenge as it is presented.

My final word on how to use this book: Please don't rush through it at the last minute. The five questions appear simple, but they are not. Give them time to sink in; wrestle over them. Properly carried through, self-assessment develops skill, competence, and commitment. Active and attentive participation is an opportunity to enhance your vision and *to shape the future*.

Definition of Terms

Mission Why you do what you do; the organization's reason for being, its purpose. Says what, in the end, you want to be remembered for.

Vision A picture of the organization's desired future.

Customers Those who must be satisfied in order for the organization to achieve results. The *primary customer* is the person whose life is changed through the organization's work. *Supporting customers* are volunteers, members, partners, funders, referral sources, employees, and others who must be satisfied.

Customer Value That which satisfies customers' *needs* (physical and psychological well-being), *wants* (where, when, and how service is provided), and *aspirations* (desired long-term results).

Results The organization's bottom line. Defined in *changed lives*—people's behavior, circumstances, health, hopes, competence, or capacity. Results are always *outside* the organization.

Goals A set of three to five aims that set the organization's fundamental, long-range direction.

Objectives Specific and measurable levels of achievement.

Action Steps Detailed plans and activities directed toward meeting an organization's objectives.

Budget The commitment of resources necessary to implement plans—the financial expression of a particular plan of work.

Appraisal Process for monitoring progress in meeting objectives and achieving results; point at which the plans for meeting objectives may be modified, based on experience or changed conditions.

There are four additional terms in the self-assessment process that may not be familiar:

Depth Interviews One-on-one interviews used to highlight the insights of a select group of individuals inside the organization. Interview findings provide a touchstone for group discussions and decision making.

Environmental Scan A process for discovering and documenting facts and trends in the operating environment that are likely to affect the organization in its future work. Environmental scan findings are used to orient self-assessment participants.

Internal Data Summarized information regarding the history, present status, and performance of the organization. Includes a current mission statement. Internal data are used to orient self-assessment participants.

Leadership Team The chairman of the board and the chief executive officer of a nonprofit organization. These leaders of the governance and management of the organization work together to make self-assessment possible.

PART TWO

The Five Questions

The 5 Most Important Questions

QUESTION 1

What is our mission?

WORKSHEETS

1. What is the current mission?

2. What are our challenges?

3. What are our opportunities?

4. Does the mission need to be revisited?

QUESTION 2 Who is our customer?

QUESTION 3 What does the customer value?

QUESTION 4 What are our results?

QUESTION 5 What is our plan?

What is our mission?

What is the current mission?
What are our challenges?
What are our opportunities?
Does the mission need to be revisited?

Each social sector institution exists to make a distinctive difference in the lives of individuals and in society. Making this difference is the mission—the organization's purpose and very reason for being. Each of more than one million nonprofit organizations in the United States may have a very different mission, but *changing lives* is always the starting point and ending point. A mission cannot be impersonal; it has to have deep meaning, be something you believe in—something you know is right. A fundamental responsibility of leadership is to make sure that everybody knows the mission, understands it, lives it.

Many years ago, I sat down with the administrators of a major hospital to think through the mission of the emergency room. As do most hospital administrators, they began by saying, "Our mission is health care." And that's the wrong definition. The hospital does not take care of heath; the hospital takes care of illness. It took us a long time to come up with the very simple and (most people thought) too-obvious statement that the emergency room was there *to give assurance to the afflicted.* To do that well, you had to know what really went on. And, to the surprise of the physicians and nurses, the function of a good emergency room in their community was to tell eight out of ten people there was nothing wrong that a good night's sleep wouldn't fix. "You've been shaken up. Or the baby has the flu. All right, it's got convulsions, but there is nothing seriously wrong with the child." The doctors and nurses gave assurance.

We worked it out, but it sounded awfully obvious. Yet translating the mission into action meant that everybody who came in was seen by a qualified person in less than a minute. The first objective was to see everybody, almost immediately—because that is the only way to give assurance.

It Should Fit on a T-Shirt

The effective mission statement is short and sharply focused. It should fit on a T-shirt. The mission says *why* you do what you do, not the means by which you do it. The mission is broad, even eternal, yet directs you to do the right things now and into the future so that everyone in the organization can say, "What I am doing contributes to the goal." So it must be clear, and it must inspire. Every board member, volunteer, and staff person should be able to see the mission and say, "Yes. This is something I want to be remembered for."

To have an effective mission, you have to work out an exacting match of your opportunities, competence, and commitment. Every good mission statement reflects all three. You look first at the outside environment. The organization that starts from the inside and then tries to find places to put its resources is going to fritter itself away. Above all, it will focus on yesterday. Demographics change. Needs change. You must search out the accomplished facts—things that have already happened—that present challenges and opportunities for the organization. Leadership has no choice but to anticipate the future and attempt to mold it, bearing in mind that whoever is content to rise with the tide will also fall with it. It is not given to mortals to do any of these things well, but, lacking divine guidance, you must still assess where your opportunity lies.

Look at the state of the art, at changing conditions, at competition, the funding environment, at gaps to be filled. The hospital isn't going to sell shoes, and it's not going into education on a big scale. It's going to take care of the sick. But the specific aim may change. Things that are of primary importance now may become secondary or totally irrelevant very soon. With the limited resources you have—and I don't just mean people and money but also competence—where can you dig in and make a difference? Where can you set a new standard of performance? What really inspires your commitment?

Why Does the Organization Exist?

Defining the nonprofit mission is difficult, painful, and risky. But it alone enables you to set goals and objectives and go to work. Unless the mission is explicitly expressed, clearly understood, and supported by every member of the organization, the enterprise is at the mercy of events. Decision makers throughout will decide and act on the basis of different, incompatible, and conflicting ideas. They will pull in opposing directions without even being aware of their divergence, and your performance is what suffers. Common vision, understanding, and unity of direction and effort of the entire organization depend on defining the mission and what the mission *should* be.

Make Principled Decisions

One cautionary note: *Never subordinate the mission in order to get money.* If there are opportunities that threaten the integrity of the organization, you must say no. Otherwise, you sell your soul. I sat in on a discussion at a museum that had been offered a donation of important art on conditions that no self-respecting museum could possibly accept. Yet a few board members said, "Let's take the donation. We can change the conditions down the road." "No, that's unconscionable!" others responded, and the board fought over the issue. They finally agreed they would lose too much by compromising basic principles to please a donor. The board forfeited some very nice pieces of sculpture, but core values had to come first.

Keep Thinking It Through

Keep the central question What is our mission? in front of you throughout the self-assessment process. Step by step you will analyze challenges and opportunities, identify your customers, learn what they value, and define your results. When it is time to develop the plan, you will take all that you have learned and revisit the mission to affirm or change it.

As you begin, consider this wonderful sentence from a sermon of that great poet and religious philosopher of the seventeenth century, John Donne: "Never start with tomorrow to reach eternity. Eternity is not being reached by small steps." We start with the long range and then feed back and say, "What do we do *today?*" The ultimate test is not the beauty of the mission statement. The ultimate test is your performance.

What is the current mission?

Write or attach a copy of the organization's current mission statement here.

What meaning does the mission have for you?

In what ways has the organization furthered the mission?

What are our challenges?

Your organization may have conducted an environmental scan to gain a picture of the organization's future context. Identify relevant challenges and their implications by using information from that scan, internal data, other information on external trends, and your own experience and insights.

Does the organization face challenges due to:

	Short term	Long term	Both	Not at this time
Changing demographics?	☐	☐	☐	☐
Changing community conditions?	☐	☐	☐	☐
Cultural or social trends?	☐	☐	☐	☐
Trends in the economy or funding environment?	☐	☐	☐	☐
Politics, legislation, or regulation?	☐	☐	☐	☐
Competition?	☐	☐	☐	☐
New technologies, models, or methods?	☐	☐	☐	☐
Other _____	☐	☐	☐	☐

Which of the challenges above are the most significant for the organization? Why?

What are our opportunities?

Challenges and opportunities are often two sides of the same coin. Refer to Worksheet 2, your organization's environmental scan, other information on external trends, and your own experience and insights to identify potential opportunities. Write them below and indicate whether they are available in the short term, the long term, or both.

	Short term	Long term	Both
What opportunities does the organization have to address compelling issues or conditions?			
Are the opportunities:	☐	☐	☐
What opportunities does the organization have to fill a gap in its area of service?			
Are the opportunities:	☐	☐	☐
What opportunities does the organization have to meet the interests of potential partners or funders?			
Are the opportunities:	☐	☐	☐
What opportunities does the organization have to be a leader, to set a new standard of performance?			
Are the opportunities:	☐	☐	☐

Which opportunities are most promising for the organization? Why?

Does the mission need to be revisited?

Rate your current mission using the following criteria, then decide whether you believe it should be changed and, if so, how.

The mission:	Yes, absolutely	To some extent	Not at all
Is short and sharply focused.	☐	☐	☐
Is clear and easily understood.	☐	☐	☐
Defines why we do what we do, why the organization exists.	☐	☐	☐
Does not prescribe means.	☐	☐	☐
Is sufficiently broad.	☐	☐	☐
Provides direction for doing the right things.	☐	☐	☐
Addresses our opportunities.	☐	☐	☐
Matches our competence.	☐	☐	☐
Inspires our commitment.	☐	☐	☐
Says what, in the end, we want to be remembered for.	☐	☐	☐
Should the mission be revisited?	☐	☐	☐

If so, what changes should be considered?

If there is agreement the mission needs to be revisited, continue to consider what the mission should be as you work through the next three self-assessment questions. The mission is revisited in a retreat or group discussion when responding to the last Drucker question, What is our plan?

The 5 Most Important Questions

QUESTION 1   What is our mission?

QUESTION 2

Who is our customer?

WORKSHEETS

5. Who are our primary and supporting customers?

6. How will our customers change?

QUESTION 3   What does the customer value?

QUESTION 4   What are our results?

QUESTION 5   What is our plan?

Who is our customer?

Who is our primary customer?
Who are our supporting customers?
How will our customers change?

Not long ago, the word *customer* was rarely heard in the social sector. Nonprofit leaders would say, "We don't have customers. That's a marketing term. We have clients . . . recipients . . . patients. We have audience members. We have students." Rather than debate language, I ask, "Who must be satisfied for the organization to achieve results?" When you answer this question, you define your customer as one who values your service, who wants what you offer, who feels it's important to *them.*

Social sector organizations have two types of customers. The *primary customer* is the person whose life is changed through your work. Effectiveness requires focus, and that means *one* response to the question, Who is our primary customer? Those who chase off in too many directions suffer by diffusing their energies and diminishing their performance. *Supporting customers* are volunteers, members, partners, funders, referral sources, employees, and others who must be satisfied. They are all people who can say no, people who have the choice to accept or reject what you offer. You might satisfy them by providing the opportunity for meaningful service, by directing contributions toward results you both believe in, by joining forces to meet community needs.

The primary customer is never the *only* customer, and to satisfy one customer without satisfying the others means there is no performance. This makes it very tempting to say there is more than one primary customer, but effective organizations resist this temptation and keep to a focus—the primary customer.

Identify the Primary Customer

Let me give you a positive example of identifying and concentrating on the primary customer in a complex setting. A mid-sized nonprofit organization's mission is *to increase people's economic and social independence.* They have twenty-five programs considered to be in four different fields, but for thirty-five years they have focused on only one primary customer: *the person with multiple barriers to employment.* In the beginning, this meant the physically handicapped. Today, it still means people with disabilities but also single mothers who want to be finished with welfare, older workers who have been laid off, people with chronic and persistent mental illness living in the community, and those struggling against long-term chemical dependency. Each belongs to a single primary customer group: the person with multiple barriers to employment. Results are measured in every program by whether the customer can now gain and keep productive work.

The primary customer is not necessarily someone you can reach, someone you can sit down with and talk to directly. Primary customers may be infants, or endangered species, or members of a future generation. Whether or not you can have an active dialogue, identifying the primary customer puts your priorities in order and gives you a reference point for critical decisions on the organization's values.

Identify Supporting Customers

The Girl Scouts of the United States of America is the largest girls' and women's organization in the world and a nonprofit that exemplifies service to one primary customer—the girl—balanced with satisfaction of many supporting customers, all of whom change over time. A long-held Girl Scouts priority is offering equal access to every girl in the United States. This has not changed since 1912 when the Girl Scouts founder said, "I have something for all the girls." Frances Hesselbein, at the time she was national executive director (1976–1990), told me, "We look at the projections and understand that by the year 2000, one-third of this country will be members of minority groups. Many people are very apprehensive about the future and what this new racial and ethnic composition will mean. We see it as an unprecedented opportunity to reach all girls with a program that will help them in their growing-up years, which are more difficult than ever before."

Reaching a changing primary customer means a new view of supporting customers. Frances explained, "In a housing project with no Girl Scout troop there are hundreds of young girls really needing this kind of program, and families wanting something better for their children. It is important as we reach out to girls in every racial and economic group to understand the very special needs, the culture, the readiness of each group. We work with many supporting customers; with the clergy perhaps, with the director of that housing project, with parents—a group of people from that particular community. We recruit leaders, train them right there. We have to demonstrate our respect for that community, our interest in it. Parents have to know it will be a positive experience for their daughters."

Know Your Customers

Customers are never static. There will be greater or lesser numbers in the groups you already serve. They will become more diverse. Their needs, wants, and aspirations will evolve. There may be entirely new customers you must satisfy to achieve results—individuals who really need the service, want the service, but not in the way in which it is available today. And there are customers you should *stop* serving because the organization has filled a need, because people can be better served elsewhere, or because you are not producing results.

Answering the question Who is our customer? provides the basis for determining what customers value, defining your results, and developing the plan. Yet, even after careful thought, customers may surprise you; then you must be prepared to adjust. I remember one of my pastoral friends saying of a new program, "Great, a wonderful program for the newly married." The program was indeed a success. But to the consternation of the young assistant pastor who designed it and ran it, not a single newly married couple enrolled. All the participants were young people living together and wondering whether they should get married. And the senior pastor had a terrible time with his brilliant young assistant, who became righteous and said, "We haven't designed it for them!" He wanted to throw them out.

Often, the customer is one step ahead of you. So you must *know your customer*—or quickly get to know them. Time and again you will have to ask, "Who is our customer?" because customers constantly change. The organization that is devoted to results—always with regard for its basic integrity—will adapt and change as they do.

Who are our primary and supporting customers?

Your primary customer is the person whose life is changed through your work. Write the organization's primary customer below. If you are unsure who *the* primary customer is, write your strongest thought here and include others as supporting customers.

Who is the primary customer?

Supporting customers are the individuals and groups who, in addition to the primary customer, must be satisfied in order for the organization to achieve results. They may include volunteers, members, partners, funders, referral sources, employees, and others. Write supporting customers below.

Who are the supporting customers?

How will our customers change?

Customer groups aren't static. The characteristics, needs, wants, and aspirations of current customers continuously evolve, and there are often entirely new customers the organization must satisfy to achieve results. Think ahead to how your customers will change. For any box you check, briefly describe the changes you believe will occur and the time frame for your projection.

Primary Customers

☐ There will be more primary customers.

    If so, what growth is projected?

☐ There will be fewer primary customers.

    If so, what loss is projected?

☐ Primary customers will become more diverse.

    If so, how?

☐ Primary customers' *needs* (physical and psychological well-being) will change.

    If so, how?

☐ Primary customers' *wants* (where, when, and how service is provided) will change.

    If so, how?

☐ Primary customers' *aspirations* (desired long-term results) will change.

    If so, how?

Supporting Customers

☐ There will be more supporting customers.

If so, what growth is projected?

Supporting Customer:

Supporting Customer:

Supporting Customer:

Supporting Customer:

☐ There will be fewer supporting customers.

If so, what loss is projected?

Supporting Customer:

Supporting Customer:

Supporting Customer:

Supporting Customer:

☐ Supporting customers will become more diverse.

If so, how?

Supporting Customer:

Supporting Customer:

Supporting Customer:

Supporting Customer:

☐ Supporting customers' *needs* (physical and psychological well-being) will change.

If so, how?

Supporting Customer:

Supporting Customer:

Supporting Customer:

Supporting Customer:

☐ Supporting customers' *wants* (where, when, and how service is provided) will change.

If so, how?

Supporting Customer:

Supporting Customer:

Supporting Customer:

Supporting Customer:

☐ Supporting customers' *aspirations* (desired long-term results) will change.

If so, how?

Supporting Customer:

Supporting Customer:

Supporting Customer:

Supporting Customer:

Primary and supporting customers make up the overall customer groups for the organization. Now consider whether they are the right groups. There may be new customers the organization must satisfy in order to further the mission and achieve results. And there may be existing customers you should stop serving because the organization has satisfied a need, because those customers can be better served elsewhere, or because you are not producing results.

Are there new customers the organization must satisfy in order to achieve results?　　　　　☐ Yes　　☐ No

If so, who are they? Why should the organization start serving them?

Should the organization stop serving any existing customers? ☐ Yes ☐ No

If so, who are they? Why should the organization stop serving them?

The 5 Most Important Questions

QUESTION 1   What is our mission?

QUESTION 2   Who is our customer?

QUESTION 3

What does the customer value?

WORKSHEETS

7. What do we believe our primary and supporting customers value?

8. What knowledge do we need to gain from our customers?

9. How will I participate in gaining this knowledge?

QUESTION 4   What are our results?

QUESTION 5   What is our plan?

What does the customer value?

What do we believe our primary and supporting customers value?
What knowledge do we need to gain from our customers?
How will I participate in gaining this knowledge?

The question, What do customers value?—what satisfies their needs, wants, and aspirations—is so complicated that it can only be answered by customers themselves. And the first rule is that there are no irrational customers. Almost without exception, customers behave rationally in terms of their own realities and their own situation. Leadership should not even try to guess at the answers but should always go to the customers in a systematic quest for those answers. I practice this. Each year I personally telephone a random sample of fifty or sixty students who graduated ten years earlier. I ask, "Looking back, what did we contribute in this school? What is still important to you? What should we do better? What should we stop doing?" And believe me, the knowledge I have gained has had a profound influence.

What does the customer value? may be the most important question. Yet it is the one least often asked. Nonprofit leaders tend to answer it for themselves. "It's the quality of our programs. It's the way we improve the community." People are so convinced they are doing the right things and so committed to their cause that they come to see the institution as an end in itself. But that's a bureaucracy. Instead of asking, "Does it deliver value to our customers?" they ask, "Does it fit our rules?" And that not only inhibits performance but also destroys vision and dedication.

Understand Your Assumptions

My friend Philip Kotler, a professor at Northwestern University, points out that many organizations are very clear about the value they would like to deliver, but they often don't understand that value from the perspective of their customers.

They make assumptions based on their own interpretation. So begin with assumptions and find out what *you* believe your customers value. Then you can compare these beliefs with what customers actually are saying, find the differences, and go on to assess your results.

What Does the Primary Customer Value?

Learning what their primary customers value led to significant change in a homeless shelter. The shelter's existing beliefs about value added up to nutritious meals and clean beds. A series of face-to-face interviews with their homeless customers was arranged, and both board and staff members took part. They found out that yes, the food and beds are appreciated but do little or nothing to satisfy the deep aspiration *not to be homeless*. The customers said, "We need a place of safety from which to rebuild our lives, a place we can at least temporarily call a real home." The organization threw out their assumptions and their old rules. They said, "How can we make this shelter a safe haven?" They eliminated the fear that comes with being turned back on the street each morning. They now make it possible to stay at the shelter quite a while, and work with individuals to find out what a rebuilt life means to them and how they can be helped to realize their goal.

The new arrangement also requires more of the customer. Before, it was enough to show up hungry. Now, to get what the customer values most, he must make a commitment. He must work on his problems and plans in order to stay on. The customer's stake in the relationship is greater, as are the organization's results.

What Do Supporting Customers Value?

Your knowledge of what primary customers value is of utmost importance. Yet the reality is, unless you understand equally what supporting customers value, you will not be able to put all the necessary pieces in place for the organization to perform. In social sector organizations there have always been a multitude of supporting customers, in some cases each with a veto power. A school principal has to satisfy teachers, the school board, community partners, the taxpayers, parents, and above all, the primary customer—the young student. The principal has six constituencies, each of which sees the school differently. Each of them is essential, each defines value differently, and each has to be satisfied at least to the point where they don't fire the principal, go on strike, or rebel.

What Will Encourage Contributors?

Knowing what supporting customers value enables nonprofit institutions to address two of today's biggest challenges. The first is to convert individuals who give money into "contributors," that is, citizens who take responsibility, neighbors who care. Philip Kotler reminds us that this requires careful identification of the appropriate sources of funds and the giving motives. What are that individual's personal reasons for giving money? To whom does he or she give? What results prompt the contributor to say, "Yes, that's what should be done. That's what deserves more of my support." What does this customer value enough to do more, to really become a partner in furthering the mission?

What Does "Making a Difference" Mean to Each Volunteer?

Then there is the second major challenge for nonprofits: to enhance community and common purpose. What nonprofits do for their volunteers may well be as important as what they do for their primary customers. The reason is that volunteers search for opportunities to make a meaningful contribution. They feel the need to do something where "I can make a difference." But again, you must discover what "making a difference" means to each volunteer and how they must be satisfied in order for them to give their commitment.

Listen to Your Customers

To formulate a successful plan you will need to understand each of your constituencies' concerns, especially what they consider results in the long term. Integrating what customers value into the institution's plan is almost an architectural process, a structural process. It's not too difficult to do once it's understood, but it's hard work. First, think through what knowledge you need to gain. Then listen to customers, accept what they value as objective fact, and make sure the customer's voice is part of your discussions and decisions, not just during this self-assessment process, but continually.

What do we believe our primary and supporting customers value?

Note what you believe your primary and supporting customers value.

Primary Customer: What you believe is valued.

Supporting Customer: What you believe is valued.

Supporting Customer:

Supporting Customer:

Supporting Customer:

What knowledge do we need to gain from our customers?

Listening to your customers is indispensable. Your beliefs may be confirmed or significantly altered when you learn directly what they value. Imagine you are face to face with the organization's customers and free to ask any question you like. Be specific about the knowledge you want to gain.

Primary Customer:

What do you want to learn from this customer? Their needs, wants, and aspirations? What is most appreciated about the organization? What the customer would like changed?

Supporting Customer:

What do you want to learn from this customer? Their needs, wants, and aspirations? What is most appreciated about the organization? What the customer would like changed?

Supporting Customer:

Supporting Customer:

Supporting Customer:

Prospective New Customer: What do you want to learn about this customer's needs, wants, and aspirations?

Prospective New Customer:

Prospective New Customer:

How will I participate in gaining this knowledge?

Your organization's Assessment Team will design a process to conduct customer research. Opportunities may be available to participate in data gathering or the discussion of findings. Check one or more ways you are willing to be involved.

I am willing to:

☐ Help decide questions to be answered through research.

☐ Help determine appropriate research approaches.

☐ Help design research tools.

☐ Provide training to volunteer researchers.

☐ Make telephone survey calls.

☐ Conduct one or more in-person interviews.

☐ Facilitate one or more focus groups.

☐ Help analyze data.

☐ Help write a report of findings.

☐ Make a presentation of findings.

☐ Attend a session in which findings are reported and discussed.

The 5 Most Important Questions

QUESTION 1   What is our mission?

QUESTION 2   Who is our customer?

QUESTION 3   What does the customer value?

QUESTION 4

What are our results?

WORKSHEETS

10. How do we define results?

11. Are we successful?

12. How should we define results?

13. What must we strengthen or abandon?

QUESTION 5   What is our plan?

What are our results?

How do we define results?
Are we successful?
How should we define results?
What must we strengthen or abandon?

The results of social sector organizations are always measured *outside* the organization in changed lives and changed conditions—in people's behavior, circumstances, health, hopes, and above all, in their competence and capacity. To further the mission, each nonprofit needs to determine what should be appraised and judged, then concentrate resources for results.

Look at Short-Term Accomplishments and Long-Term Change

A small mental health center was founded and directed by a dedicated husband-and-wife team, both psychotherapists. They called it a "healing community," and in the fifteen years they ran the organization, they achieved results others had dismissed as impossible. Their primary customers were people diagnosed with schizophrenia, and most came to the center following failure after failure in treatment, their situation nearly hopeless.

The people at the center said, "There *is* somewhere to turn." Their first measure was whether primary customers and their families were willing to try again. The staff had a number of ways to monitor progress. Did participants regularly attend group sessions and participate fully in daily routines? Did the incidence and length of psychiatric hospitalizations decrease? Could these individuals show new understanding of their disease by saying, "I have had an episode," as opposed to citing demons in the closet? As they progressed, could participants set realistic goals for their own next steps?

The center's mission was *to enable people with serious and persistent mental illness to recover,* and after two or more years of intensive work, many could function in this world—they were no longer "incurable." Some were able to return to a life with their family. Others could hold steady jobs. A few completed graduate school. Whether or not members of that healing community did recover—whether the lives of primary customers changed in this fundamental way—was the organization's single bottom line.

In business, you can debate whether profit is really an adequate measuring stick, but without it, there *is* no business in the long term. In the social sector, no such universal standard for success exists. Each organization must identify its customers, learn what they value, develop meaningful measures, and honestly judge whether, in fact, lives are being changed. This is a new discipline for many non-profit groups, but it is one that can be learned.

Qualitative and Quantitative Measures

Progress and achievement can be appraised in *qualitative* and *quantitative* terms. These two types of measures are interwoven—they shed light on one another—and both are necessary to illuminate in what ways and to what extent lives are being changed.

Qualitative measures address the depth and breadth of change within its particular context. They begin with specific observations, build toward patterns, and tell a subtle, individualized story. Qualitative appraisal offers valid, "rich" data. The education director at a major museum tells of the man who sought her out to explain how the museum had opened his teenage mind to new possibilities in a way he knew literally saved his life. She used this result to support her inspiration for a new initiative with troubled youth. The people in a successful research institute cannot quantify the value of their research ahead of time. But they can sit down every three years and ask, "What have we achieved that contributed to changed lives? Where do we focus now for results tomorrow?" Qualitative results can be in the realm of the intangible, such as instilling hope in a patient battling cancer. Qualitative data, although sometimes more subjective and difficult to grasp, are just as real, just as important, and can be gathered just as systematically as the quantitative.

Quantitative measures use definitive standards. They begin with categories and expectations and tell an objective story. Quantitative appraisal offers valid "hard" data. Examples of quantitative measures are as follows: whether overall school performance improves when at-risk youth have intensive arts education; whether the percentage of welfare recipients who complete training and become employed at a livable wage goes up; whether health professionals change their practice based on new research; whether the number of teenagers who smoke goes up or down; whether incidences of child abuse fall when twenty-four-hour crisis care is available. Quantitative measures are essential for assessing whether resources are properly concentrated for results, whether progress is being made, whether lives and communities are changing for the better.

How *Should* the Organization Define Results?

What should be measured and monitored? What are the meaningful criteria for us? What are the prerequisites for success? These are the questions most often raised when I work with social sector organizations to define results. To decide, you return to the mission. You take into account your capabilities, the environment in which you work, the best studies and examples in your field. You listen carefully to primary customers and apply your knowledge of who they are and what they value. You think qualitatively and quantitatively. You work through this discipline until you are resolved on the bottom line and can therefore determine what in your organization must be appraised and judged.

Here are five examples of decisions on what results should be.

Mission: To prevent the spread of AIDS.

Results: The shift in attitude from "AIDS is something that happens to other people" to acceptance of personal responsibility; people in targeted population groups change their sexual behavior; the number of new cases of AIDS drops.

Mission (for a school): To develop contributing citizens.

Results: Students read by the end of second grade; students are constructive team members and respectful in peer relationships; graduates go on to advanced education or make a smooth transition to employment; graduates are active citizens who make a difference in their communities or beyond.

Mission (for a United Way): To unite people in building caring, vibrant communities.

Results: The most vulnerable are safe and supported; human services are well resourced and cooperatively strengthen communities, families, and individuals; economic and social disparities are reduced; priority community problems and issues are identified and overcome.

Mission: To develop a healthy nation.

Results: 100,000 new housing units are built in three years; the birthrate is controlled;

Mission: To eliminate deaths from domestic violence.

air pollution declines; free and democratic elections are held.

Results: Community leaders make observable commitments; changes in law enforcement practices and the actions of community institutions change the behaviors of both potential victims and perpetrators; there is a significant reduction in domestic violence homicides.

Concentrate Resources for Success

Success is realized through concentration, not by splintering. That enormous organization, the Salvation Army, concentrates on only four or five programs. Its executives have the courage to say, "This is not for us. Other people do it better" or "This is not where we can make the greatest contribution. It does not really fit the strength we have." Success is judged, for example, by the percentage of alcoholics restored to mental and physical health, the number of offenders who stay out of prison, how quickly and completely food kitchens and temporary shelters provide relief at the scene of a disaster.

The most exciting thing to me in almost fifty years of work with nonprofit organizations is that we no longer talk of the *need* but of success in achieving results. To believe that whatever we do is a moral cause and should be pursued whether there is success or not is a perennial temptation for nonprofit executives—and even more for their boards. Everything is "the Lord's work" or "a good cause," but we cannot afford to continue where we seem unable to further the mission. There are exceptions—those who labor in the wilderness, the true believers who are devoted to a cause and to whom success, failure, and results are irrelevant. We need such people. They are our conscience. But very few of them achieve. Nonprofit organizations are asking, "Have we been successful?" and it's high time they did.

Assess What Must Be Strengthened or Abandoned

One of the most important questions for nonprofit leadership is, Do we produce results that are sufficiently outstanding for us to justify putting our resources in this area? Need alone does not justify continuing. Nor does tradition. You must match your mission, your concentration, and your results. Like the New Testament parable of the talents, your job is to invest your resources where the returns are manifold, where you can have success.

To abandon anything is always bitterly resisted. People in any organization are always attached to the obsolete—the things that should have worked but did not, the things that once were productive and no longer are. They are most attached to what in an earlier book (*Managing for Results,* 1964) I called "investments in managerial ego." Yet abandonment comes first. Until that has been accomplished, little else gets done. The acrimonious and emotional debate over what to abandon holds everybody in its grip. Abandoning anything is thus difficult, but only for a fairly short spell. Rebirth can begin once the dead are buried; six months later, everybody wonders, "Why did it take us so long?"

Leadership Is Accountable

If essential performance areas are weak, they must be strengthened. But even then, you must consider "the unthinkable." In one international nonprofit I know of, a highly successful training program had, over thirty years, made a profound difference in health care practices for an entire nation. With an elaborate trans-Pacific infrastructure in place—and a handsome but overly specific endowment supporting it—today's leadership had to address the fact that the training strategy could no longer make a difference for the future and to begin dismantling it in favor of unproved innovations.

There are times to face the fact that the organization as a whole is not performing—that there are weak results everywhere and little prospect of improving. It may be time to merge or to liquidate and put your energies somewhere else. And in some performance areas, whether to strengthen or abandon is not clear. You will need a systematic analysis as part of your plan.

At this point in the self-assessment process, you determine what results for the organization should be and where to concentrate for future success. The mission defines the scope of your responsibility. Leadership is accountable to determine what must be appraised and judged, to protect the organization from squandering resources, and to ensure meaningful results.

How do we define results?

Results are always measured outside the organization in changed lives and changed conditions— in people's behavior, circumstances, health, hopes, competence, and capacity. What does the organization currently appraise and judge? How does it define and measure results?

How does the organization currently define results?

How does the organization monitor progress and achievement?

What results are currently being achieved?

Are we successful?

Success is defined by furthering the mission and achieving meaningful results. How successful is the organization in the eyes of its customers? How successful do you believe the organization is?

Based on what primary customers value, the organization is:

☐ Very successful ☐ Somewhat successful ☐ Not very successful ☐ Not at all successful

Comments:

Based on what supporting customers value, the organization is:

Supporting Customer:

☐ Very successful ☐ Somewhat successful ☐ Not very successful ☐ Not at all successful

Comments:

Supporting Customer:

☐ Very successful ☐ Somewhat successful ☐ Not very successful ☐ Not at all successful

Comments:

Supporting Customer:

☐ Very successful   ☐ Somewhat successful   ☐ Not very successful   ☐ Not at all successful

Comments:

Supporting Customer:

☐ Very successful   ☐ Somewhat successful   ☐ Not very successful   ☐ Not at all successful

Comments:

I believe the organization is:

☐ Very successful   ☐ Somewhat successful   ☐ Not very successful   ☐ Not at all successful

Comments:

How should we define results?

The determination of what the organization's future results should be is a critical decision that will greatly influence your plan. What should be the organization's results in changed lives?

How should the organization define results for the future?

How should the organization monitor progress and achievement?

What must we strengthen or abandon?

In most organizations, there are programs requiring special attention. They may be strong and ready to grow, weak and in need of improvement, or "candidates for abandonment." If you have questions about an area but aren't prepared to make a judgment, mark it for analysis. Internal systems such as financial development, human resource management, marketing, or operations may also require special attention. Note internal areas where performance should be assessed.

Programs in need of attention   Strengthen   Abandon   Analyze

Internal systems that should be assessed   Reason for assessment

The 5 Most Important Questions

QUESTION 1   What is our mission?

QUESTION 2   Who is our customer?

QUESTION 3   What does the customer value?

QUESTION 4   What are our results?

QUESTION 5

What is our plan?

WORKSHEETS

14. Should the mission be changed?

15. What are our goals?

What is our plan?

Should the mission be changed?
What are our goals?

Get the Right Things Done

The self-assessment process leads to a plan that is a concise summation of the organization's purpose and future direction. The plan encompasses mission, vision, goals, objectives, action steps, a budget, and appraisal. Now comes the point to affirm or change the mission and set long-range goals. Remember, every mission statement has to reflect three things: opportunities, competence, and commitment. It answers the questions, *What is our purpose? Why do we do what we do? What, in the end, do we want to be remembered for?* The mission transcends today but guides today, informs today. It provides the framework for setting goals and mobilizing the resources of the organization for getting the right things done.

The development and formal adoption of mission and goals are fundamental to effective governance of a nonprofit organization and are primary responsibilities of the board. Therefore, these strategic elements of the plan must be approved by the board.

To further the mission, there must be action today and specific aims for tomorrow. Yet planning is not masterminding the future. Any attempt to do so is foolish; the future is unpredictable. In the face of uncertainties, planning defines the particular place you *want* to be and how you intend to get there. Planning does not substitute facts for judgment nor science for leadership. It recognizes the importance of analysis, courage, experience, intuition—even hunch. It is responsibility rather than technique.

Goals Are Few, Overarching, and Approved by the Board

The most difficult challenge is to agree on the institution's goals—the fundamental long-range direction. Goals are overarching and should be few in number. If you have more than five goals, you have none. You're simply spreading yourself too thin. Goals make it absolutely clear where you will concentrate resources for results—the mark of an organization serious about success. Goals flow from mission, aim the organization where it must go, build on strength, address opportunity, and taken together, outline your desired future.

An option for the plan is a vision statement picturing a future when the organization's goals are achieved and its mission accomplished. The Drucker Foundation's vision is: *A society that recognizes the social sector as the leading force in creating healthy communities and improving the quality of life.* I have worked with groups who became intensely motivated by these often-idealistic and poetic statements, whereas others say, "Let's not get carried away." If a vision statement—whether a sentence or a page—helps bring the plan to life, by all means include it.

Here is an example of the vision, mission, and goals for an art museum.

Vision   A city where the world's diverse artistic heritage is prized and whose people seek out art to feed their mind and spirit.

Mission   To bring art and people together.

Goal 1   To conserve the collections and inspire partnerships to seek and acquire exceptional objects.

Goal 2   To enable people to discover, enjoy, and understand art through popular and scholarly exhibitions, community education, and publications.

Goal 3   To significantly expand the museum's audience and strengthen its impact with new and traditional members.

Goal 4   To maintain state-of-the-art facilities, technologies, and operations.

Goal 5   To enhance long-term financial security.

Building around mission and long-term goals is the only way to integrate shorter-term interests. Then management can always ask, "Is an objective leading us toward our basic long-range goal, or is it going to sidetrack us, divert us, make us lose sight of our aims?" St. Augustine said, "One prays for miracles but works for results." Your plan leads you to work for results. It converts intentions into action.

Objectives Are Measurable, Concrete, and the Responsibility of Management

Objectives are the specific and measurable levels of achievement that move the organization toward its goals. The chief executive officer is responsible for development of objectives and the action steps and detailed budgets that follow. The board must not act at the level of tactical planning, or it interferes with management's vital ability to be flexible in how goals are achieved. When developing and implementing a plan, the board is accountable for mission, goals, and the allocation of resources to results, and for appraising progress and achievement. Management is accountable for objectives, for action steps, for the supporting budget, as well as for demonstrating effective performance.

Five Elements of Effective Plans

Abandonment

The first decision is whether to abandon what does not work, what has never worked—the things that have outlived their usefulness and their capacity to contribute. Ask of any program, system, or customer group, "If we were not committed to this today, would we go into it?" If the answer is no, say "How can we get out—fast?"

Concentration

Concentration is building on success, strengthening what *does* work. The best rule is to put your efforts into your successes. You will get maximum results. When you have strong performance is the very time to ask, "Can we set an even higher standard?" Concentration is vital, but it's also very risky. You must choose the right concentrations, or—to use a military term—you leave your flanks totally uncovered.

Innovation

You must also look for tomorrow's success, the true innovations, the diversity that stirs the imagination. What are the opportunities, the new conditions, the emerging issues? Do they fit you? Do you really believe in this? But you have to be careful. Before you go into something new, don't say, "This is how we do it." Say, "Let's find out what this requires. What does the customer value? What is the state of the art? How can we make a difference?" Finding answers to these questions is essential.

Risk taking

Planning always involves decisions on where to take the risks. Some risks you can afford to take—if something goes wrong, it is easily reversible with minor damage. And some decisions may carry great risk, but you cannot afford *not* to take it. You have to balance the short range with the long. If you are too conservative, you miss the opportunity. If you commit too much too fast, there may not be a long run to worry about. There is no formula for these risk-taking decisions. They are entrepreneurial and uncertain, but they must be made.

Analysis

Finally, in planning it is important to recognize when you do *not* know, when you are not yet sure whether to abandon, concentrate, go into something new, or take a particular risk. Then your objective is to conduct an analysis. Before making the final decision, you study a weak but essential performance area, a challenge on the horizon, the opportunity just beginning to take shape.

Build Understanding and Ownership

The plan begins with a mission. It ends with *action steps* and a *budget*. Action steps establish accountability for objectives—who will do what by when—and the budget commits the resources necessary to implement the plan. To build understanding and ownership for the plan, action steps are developed by the people who will carry them out. Everyone with a role should have the opportunity to give input. This looks incredibly slow. But when the plan is completed, the next day everyone understands it. More people in the organization want the new, are committed to it, are ready to act.

The Assessment Team will prepare the final plan for review by the board. Following presentation and discussion, the board chairman will request approval of the mission, goals, and supporting budget. The chairman may request adoption of a vision statement, if one has been developed, as part of the plan. As soon as approval is given, implementation begins.

This is the last of the self-assessment questions, and your involvement as a participant soon draws to a close. Appraisal will be ongoing. The organization must monitor progress in achieving goals and meeting objectives, and above all, must measure results in changed lives. You must adjust the plan when conditions change, results are poor, there is a surprise success, or when the customer leads you to a place different from where you imagined.

True self-assessment is never finished. Leadership requires that constant resharpening, refocusing, never really being satisfied. I encourage you especially to keep asking the question, *What do we want to be remembered for?* It is a question that induces you to renew yourself—and the organization—because it pushes you to see what you can become.

Planning for Results Diagram

Mission is essential to social sector planning. The mission answers the questions: What is the organization's purpose? Why does it exist? From the mission flow *goals* that set the organization's fundamental long-range direction and, together, outline its desired future. *Objectives* are specific and measurable levels of achievement. *Action steps* are the detailed plans and activities to meet the objectives; the *budget* commits necessary resources; and *appraisal* demonstrates whether objectives are met and *results* achieved. The illustration uses a circular movement to show that evaluation—and planning—is continuous.

Should the mission be changed?

Mission reflects the institution's opportunities, competence, and commitment. The mission answers the questions, *What is our purpose? Why do we do what we do? What, in the end, do we want to be remembered for?* On Worksheet 4, you considered whether the mission should be revisited. Return to Worksheet 4, review your earlier work, and decide whether you now believe the mission should be changed. If so, write your recommendation for what the mission should be.

Should the mission be changed?　　☐　Yes　　☐　No

What should the mission be?

What are our goals?

Your understanding of what the mission should be is also expressed by recommending goals that set the organization's overarching long-term direction. Goals are few in number to ensure the concentration of resources for results, and together outline the organization's desired future.

What should the organization's goals be?

1.

2.

3.

4.

5.

Afterword: Effective Implementation of the Plan

Work doesn't get done by a magnificent statement of policy. Work is only done when it's done. Done by people. By people who are properly informed, assigned, and equipped. People with a deadline. People who are developed and evaluated. The best plan is *only* a plan—a set of good intentions—unless there is communication, action, appraisal, and the continuous reallocation of the organization's resources to getting results. The immediate test of a plan is whether leadership actually commits resources to its implementation. Unless such commitment is made, there are only promises and hopes—but no plan.

Communication, Development of People, and Performance

The nonprofit organization must be information-based. Information must flow from the individuals doing the work to the board and management, and it must flow back as well. In a national voluntary organization, the day after the board approved their plan, the chairman was off on a round of visits to local chapters. At each stop she met with leaders and gave speeches focused on mission, vision, goals, and how the local chapter could contribute to results. She answered question after question from individual members and encouraged them to communicate their experience and observations directly to national leadership as time went on. Simultaneously, the executive director held meetings with staff, confirmed new assignments, and led discussion on objectives, action steps, and how progress and achievement would be appraised. The board chairman and chief executive immediately demonstrated their commitment to the plan and set the stage for ongoing communication.

Management emphasis should always be on performance. But, especially for a nonprofit organization, it must also be on developing people. Staff and volunteers require clear assignments that tap their strengths and allow them—through training, encouragement, and the right challenges—to expand these strengths. They need frequent and open opportunities to review team and individual performance. They need leaders and managers who sit down and say, "This is what you and I committed ourselves to. How have we done? What should we do to further your growth?" The guideline is, if people try, work with them. Look for a different way they can contribute. But if a person cannot perform, another assignment should be considered. The alternative is that all those who have to work with the person lose their capacity to contribute. Without management resolve in these difficult situations, the plan becomes hollow.

Appraisal Is All-Important

What we measure and how we measure it determines what will be considered relevant and thereby determines not just what we see but what we—and others—do. Monitoring should be built in early, involve people at all levels of the organization, and give leadership the ability to quickly take corrective action or move to build on success. There must be systematic feedback—a way of self-control from events back to planning.

Your plan commits present resources to the uncertainties of the future. This, according to elementary probability mathematics, means some decisions will prove to be wrong. Adjusting them requires two things: first, that you think through alternatives ahead of time so that you have something to fall back on; and second, that you build into the plan the responsibility for bailing it out instead of arguing about who made what mistakes.

When a new tactic or action doesn't seem to be working, the rule is, "If at first you don't succeed, try once more." Stop and ask what has been learned. Try to improve the strategy, to change it, and make another major effort. Maybe, although I am reluctant to encourage it, you should make a third effort. After that, go to work where the results are.

Appraisal should not focus on flaws and mistakes at the expense of achievement. There is a tendency to devote the most time to problem solving, to pour more and more into rescuing a failure. When you have results, communicate them, give recognition where it is due, and reward effectiveness. Take time to analyze what has gone *right,* how even better results might be achieved, how success in one area can be translated to others.

At the same time, bear in mind that no success is forever. It is far more difficult to abandon yesterday's success than it is to reappraise failure. Success breeds its own hubris. It creates emotional attachment, habits of mind and action, and, above all, false self-confidence. A success that has outlived its usefulness—and today this happens very quickly—may, in the end, be more damaging than failure.

Mission Is the Star to Steer By

A plan is a framework, not a formula. When conditions change, when complex decisions must be made, first ask, "What will further the mission?" Then look to goals, to what results should and *could* be. The greatest mistake when implementing a plan is to allow objectives to become a straitjacket; commitment to mission and goals is long term, but one always makes compromises on tactics.

I know of a public health organization that was approached by a school system asking for a partnership, a means for that public health organization to take a prevention program directly into the classroom and reach children—the primary customers—quickly and in great numbers. They struggled over the opportunity because "it wasn't in the plan," and their people were already working on a different approach. It took open minds and managerial agility to change direction, to take the entrepreneurial risk and abandon an objective mid-course in favor of a more effective one.

My hope, as you complete this formal process, is that you do not stop with "what is in the plan" but make true self-assessment an ongoing practice. This means constant scanning of the environment, continual learning from the customer. It means appraisal, countless small adjustments, and the courage to make major change. True self-assessment creates, through dedication and hard work, that flow of knowledge throughout the organization that strengthens judgment, renews leadership, and inspires vision. It is the foundation of excellence in performance.

About the Drucker Foundation

The Peter F. Drucker Foundation for Nonprofit Management, founded in 1990, takes its name and inspiration from the acknowledged father of modern management. By providing educational opportunities and resources, the foundation furthers its mission "to lead social sector organizations toward excellence in performance." It pursues this mission through the presentation of conferences, video teleconferences, the annual Peter F. Drucker Award for Nonprofit Innovation, and the annual Frances Hesselbein Community Innovation Fellows Program, as well as through the development of management resources, partnerships, and publications.

Since its founding, the Drucker Foundation's special role has been to serve as a broker of intellectual capital, bringing together the finest leaders, consultants, authors, and social philosophers in the world with the leaders of social sector voluntary organizations.

The Drucker Foundation believes that a healthy society requires three vital sectors: a public sector of effective governments, a private sector of effective businesses, and a social sector of effective community organizations. The mission of the social sector and its organizations is to change lives. It accomplishes this mission by addressing the needs of the spirit, mind, and body of individuals, the community, and society. This sector and its organizations also create a meaningful sphere of effective and responsible citizenship.

The Drucker Foundation aims to make its contribution to the health of society by strengthening the social sector through the provision of intellectual resources to leaders in business, government, and the social sector. In the first seven years after its inception, the Drucker Foundation, among other things:

- Presented the Drucker Innovation Award, which each year generates several hundred applications from local community enterprises; many applicants work in fields where results are difficult to achieve.

- Held twenty conferences in the United States and in countries across the world.

- Developed four books; three books in the Drucker Foundation Future Series are *The Leader of the Future* (1996), *The Organization of the Future* (1997), and *The Community of the Future* (1998).

- Developed *Leader to Leader,* a quarterly journal for leaders from all three sectors.
- Assisted in the development of similar organizations in Argentina and Canada.

If you would like more information on the Drucker Foundation and its programs and publications, please write, call, FAX, or e-mail the foundation at:

The Peter F. Drucker Foundation for Nonprofit Management
320 Park Avenue, 3rd Floor
New York, NY 10022-6839
Telephone: (212) 224-1174
Fax: (212) 224-2508
E-mail: info@pfdf.org
Web address: www.pfdf.org

The foundation's Web site includes dates and locations of self-assessment training workshops, and additional resources to inform and guide Assessment Teams and participants.

Self-Assessment Tool
Customer Feedback Form

This revised edition of *The Drucker Foundation Self-Assessment Tool* was produced with significant input from our customers. Your feedback as a customer is very important in appraising the success of the *Tool,* in determining how it can best be introduced to others, and in considering new resources the Drucker Foundation might offer. We hope you will take a few minutes to complete the survey and return it to us by mail or fax. You can also complete this survey on our Web site at www.pfdf.org.

I. Tell us about your organization.

1. Year founded: _____

2. Annual operating budget:
   - ☐ Less than $100,000
   - ☐ $100,001 to $500,000
   - ☐ $500,001 to $2,000,000
   - ☐ $2,000,001 to $10,000,000
   - ☐ More than $10,000,000

3. Is your organization a
   - ☐ Nonprofit
   - ☐ Unit of government
   - ☐ For-profit business

4. In which area or areas does your organization work? (Check as many as apply.)
   - ☐ Arts, culture
   - ☐ Community development
   - ☐ Education
   - ☐ Employment/job opportunities
   - ☐ Environment
   - ☐ Health
   - ☐ Human service
   - ☐ Management training/consulting
   - ☐ Philanthropic/foundation
   - ☐ Religious/spiritual
   - ☐ Youth service
   - ☐ Other _____

5. Which best describes your organization's service area?
   - ☐ Urban center
   - ☐ Suburban area
   - ☐ Small town
   - ☐ Metropolitan area
   - ☐ Region
   - ☐ State
   - ☐ Nation
   - ☐ International
   - ☐ Other _____

6. Does your organization primarily serve an ethnic, racial, or culturally specific constituency?

   ☐ Yes   ☐ No

   If yes, please identify constituency:

II. Tell us about your experience with the *Self-Assessment Tool.*

7. How did you first hear about *The Drucker Foundation Self-Assessment Tool?*

   ☐ In mailings from the publisher (Jossey-Bass)
   ☐ At a self-assessment training workshop
   ☐ At a conference
   ☐ By word of mouth
   ☐ Read an article or review about it
   ☐ Saw an advertisement for it
   ☐ At Drucker Foundation Web site
   ☐ Other _____

8. How have you used the *Self-Assessment Tool?* (Check as many as apply.)

   ☐ Read the materials
   ☐ Used one or more exercises
   ☐ Applied the ideas or concepts in my work
   ☐ Conducted a self-assessment process
   ☐ Other _____

If your organization did not conduct a self-assessment process, please skip to question 11.

9. In your organization's self-assessment process, did you use a facilitator?

   ☐ No
   ☐ Yes, we used an outside facilitator
   ☐ Yes, we used a facilitator from inside the organization
   ☐ Yes, we used both outside and inside facilitators

10. Do you agree or disagree with the following statements:

The *Self-Assessment Tool* helped us:	Agree	Agree somewhat	Disagree
a. Structure and complete an organizational planning process.	☐	☐	☐
b. Identify our customers.	☐	☐	☐
c. Determine what our customers value.	☐	☐	☐
d. Clarify our organizational goals.	☐	☐	☐
e. Define what our results should be.	☐	☐	☐
f. Determine how we will measure results.	☐	☐	☐
g. Deepen understanding of our mission.	☐	☐	☐
h. Develop common vision and unity of direction.	☐	☐	☐

11. Are there any other comments you would like to make about the *Self-Assessment Tool,* about its Process Guide or Participant Workbook, or about your organization's experience with it?

III. Tell us about you.

Name _____

Organization _____

Address _____

City _____ State _____ Zip _____

Telephone _____ Fax _____ E-mail _____

12. Would you be willing to be listed in a Drucker Foundation database of organizations that have used the *Self-Assessment Tool,* and to share your experience with others?

☐ Yes   ☐ No

13. Would your organization be interested in sponsoring a Drucker Foundation Self-Assessment Training Workshop in your area?

☐ Yes   ☐ No

14. Would you be willing to participate in future customer surveys on the *Tool*?

    ☐ Yes   ☐ No

15. Would you like to be added to our mailing list for information on our publications, conferences, and resources?

    ☐ Yes   ☐ No

16. Would you or another individual who facilitated self-assessment with your organization like to be listed in a Drucker Foundation database of facilitators? The Drucker Foundation does not certify or endorse self-assessment facilitators.

    ☐ Yes   ☐ No

    Name of facilitator _____

    Organization _____

    Address _____

    City _____ State _____ Zip _____

    Telephone _____ Fax _____ E-mail _____

For information, readings, and resources, see the Drucker Foundation Web site at www.pfdf.org. Please return this form to:

The Drucker Foundation
320 Park Avenue, 3rd Floor
New York, NY 10022-6839 USA

Telephone: (212) 224-1174

Fax: (212) 224-2508

E-mail: info@pfdf.org

Web address: www.pfdf.org